The Living Splendour of Westminster Abbey

JOHN AUSTIN BAKER, *Canon of Westminster*

PUBLISHED BY JARROLD & SONS LIMITED, NORWICH
FOR THE DEAN AND CHAPTER OF WESTMINSTER

THE BEGINNINGS OF WESTMINSTER ABBEY

London as we know it today has grown up around not just one centre but two. In the east lies the ancient city of London proper, the Roman Londinium, with the Tower and St Paul's Cathedral and the world-famous 'square mile' of great commercial and financial houses. But a mile upstream is Westminster, also a city in its own right. Here are to be found the headquarters of the monarchy – Buckingham Palace, the Sovereign's official residence in the capital, and St James's Palace; the Houses of Parliament and all the chief Departments of State; the War Office, Admiralty and Air Ministry; art galleries, museums, concert halls; the 'West End' with its shops, theatres and hotels; and the head offices of many great commercial enterprises and professional organisations. At the heart of this city stands one of the most ancient and celebrated shrines of Christendom: the Collegiate Church of St Peter, known all over the world as Westminster Abbey.

It is now more than 900 years since Edward the Confessor, King and Saint, built the first church on this site. Of that building nothing now remains. In the middle of the thirteenth century King Henry III pulled it down and began the present church, completing the apse, transepts and choir, with a magnificent shrine as a new resting-place for the body of the Confessor. It was to be another 250 years before the nave was finished. Next, the Lady Chapel, the ultimate glory of English Perpendicular architecture, was begun at the east end by King Henry VII, by whose name it is generally known, and completed about 1519. Finally, the twin western towers, the feature by which the Abbey is now instantly recognised, were added in 1745, with outstanding architectural imagination and sensitivity, by Nicholas Hawksmoor, who refined and improved a design projected earlier by Sir Christopher Wren.

But if the Abbey, like many great churches, took a long time to reach its present form, growing by fits and starts, yet the life that went on within it was vigorous and continuous. As the word 'minster' in the name shows, it began as the church of a monastery. In the marshy area on the northern margin of the Thames was an island known as Thorney (meaning 'Isle of Thorns'), and a community of monks seems already to have settled here in the tenth century. This island Edward chose for his great new church, constructed in the Romanesque, round-arch style which he had admired in Normandy; and it was dedicated to St Peter on the Feast of the Holy Innocents, 28 December 1065, shortly before the King's own

The South-West Tower seen from the Deanery courtyard. For the upper part Nicholas Hawksmoor simplified and improved a design prepared by Sir Christopher Wren.

La tour sud-ouest de la cour du doyenné. La partie supérieure, de Nicholas Hawksmoor, est la version simplifiée et améliorée d'un plan de Sir Christopher Wren.

Der Südwestturm vom Dekanatshof aus gesehen. Für den oberen Teil vereinfachte und verbesserte Nicholas Hawksmoor einen von Sir Christopher Wren entworfenen Plan.

3

death. The monks later fostered a legend that there had been a church of the same dedication on the site 400 years earlier, in the time of Mellitus first Bishop of London. According to the tale, on the night before its consecration a stranger appeared on the Lambeth shore, and asked a local fisherman to ferry him over. While waiting for his passenger to return, the fisherman saw the new church ablaze with light and heard voices of a great choir. Then all went dark. When the stranger came back, he revealed himself as St Peter, and commanded the fisherman to tell Mellitus that the church was already consecrated. The story has this much historical value, that it expresses the long-standing rivalry between Westminster and St Paul's (which still survives in a friendly way today!) and the determination of the Abbey to insist on its independence of local church authority, of which more anon.

Edward's patronage – he built a royal residence hard by, his 'Palace of Westminster', which is still the official name for the complex of buildings including Westminster Hall and the Houses of Parliament across the road – and the lands with which he endowed the Abbey made it a place of growing wealth and importance. By the time of Domesday Book (1086) it was one of the ten greatest English monasteries. (None of these ancient estates remains in the Abbey's possession today, and it depends on gifts and tourism for 80 per cent of its income.)

The link with the monarchy continued after the Norman Conquest. William the Conqueror was crowned King of England in the Confessor's church on Christmas Day, 1066; and the Abbey has been the coronation church ever since. This association with the centres of power was greatly intensified after Henry III's devotion to the Confessor led him to begin the present building. Around the Confessor's Shrine Henry III himself, Edward I, Edward III, Richard II and Henry V are all buried. In the Chapter House (completed in 1253) not only did the monks gather daily under the presidency of the Abbot, but the King's Great Council of State also held its meetings; and from the time of Edward I until the end of the reign of Henry VIII it was the place of assembly for the House of Commons. Abbots of Westminster occasionally emerge as important political figures. Outstanding was Cardinal Simon Langham (tomb, pp. 40–1), whose lavish gifts and bequests paid for a considerable extension of the unfinished nave. He was Treasurer of the Royal Exchequer in 1360, before being promoted Bishop of Ely and then Archbishop of Canterbury and Lord Chancellor. But we must not exaggerate; such eminence was rare. It was not so much what Westminster Abbey did in these first centuries of its life as what it was and where it was which laid the foundations of its later unique place in the story of the nation.

The impact of such a church and its monastery on ordinary people was widespread and in some ways dramatic. It is hard for us today, when our great abbeys and cathedrals are surrounded by buildings even more massive than themselves, to imagine what it must have meant to the dwellers in the mean hovels, pokey houses and narrow streets of a medieval

4

town to enter such churches. The stained glass, the arcaded walls filled with paintings and sculpture, the gilded altars, colour and magnificence everywhere, and most of all their soaring height (from the floor of the Nave to the crown of the vault of the Abbey is 103 feet, which makes it the tallest medieval interior in England) must have struck the visitor as a foretaste of the splendour of heaven itself.

A major monastery such as Westminster was also a very considerable social and economic institution. Not only did it own vast estates; it was itself a small town within a town. The Rule of St Benedict – Westminster was a Benedictine community – had laid down as a matter of principle that 'the monastery should, if possible, be so arranged that all necessary things such as water, mill, garden and various crafts may be within the enclosure, so that the monks may not be compelled to wander outside it, for that is not at all expedient for their souls.' Hence by the time of the Reformation in the sixteenth century Westminster had range upon range of ancillary buildings: its own mill and stables, market garden, orchard and fishponds; almshouses for the poor; a grammar school and library; and, most contentious but at the same time most valued of all, a sanctuary building where criminals of every kind could find refuge from their pursuers. (The memory of this still survives in the street names of The Sanctuary and Broad Sanctuary for the areas outside and opposite the Great West Door.) Once someone on the run had crossed the River Tyburn, whose course followed what is now Great Smith Street, and passed through the gatehouse, then, so long as he remained within the Precincts, he was safe. In practice this meant that the Abbey became a base for desperadoes, which was a severe embarrassment to the church's authorities; and the right of sanctuary was eventually abolished by law. But it is one particularly dramatic illustration of the ways in which Westminster affected the lives of ordinary people.

Under Henry VIII this whole way of life was drastically changed. The monastery, in common with all others in England, was dissolved and stripped of its treasures. Then, for ten brief years (1540–50) the Abbey became a cathedral, the seat of a Bishop of Westminster, at the end of which period the new diocese was absorbed into London. But this interlude had meant that, as with all cathedrals, the administration of the church was vested in a Dean, assisted by a Chapter of Canons or Prebendaries; and after a short-lived revival of the monastery under the Roman Catholic Queen Mary I, this was continued as its method of government, Elizabeth I in 1559, soon after her coronation, establishing it by royal charter as a College or Collegiate Church.

Under this charter the Abbey became what is known as a 'royal peculiar', that is, a free chapel of the Sovereign, over which only the King or Queen for the time being has any ecclesiastical jurisdiction. The Precincts form part of no diocese; and neither the Bishop of London nor the Archbishop of Canterbury has any legal rights over or within the church. Indeed, on the first occasion when a new Archbishop of Canterbury or Bishop of London attends the Abbey in an official capacity he is required to listen to a formal 'Protest' read out by the Legal Secretary of the Dean and Chapter, reminding him that he is admitted only by their courtesy; and his own Chancellor has to reply, making formal acknowledgment of this fact. This ceremony used to take place publicly at the Great West Door, but nowadays is performed in private in the Jerusalem Chamber – needless to say, in a thoroughly amicable and social manner! But though this may seem a quaint archaic survival, the freedom which it maintains is one which, used responsibly, can enable the Abbey to take valuable initiatives in the life of church and nation which are more difficult for other institutions.

Since this new foundation by Elizabeth I set the course on which the Abbey has sailed for the last 400 years, the Collegiate Church has seen many vicissitudes which there is not space to describe fully here. But as most of them have left their mark on the building and its rich and fascinating contents, we shall be able to mention the most important as we look at these in more detail. Before doing so, however, it may help to know something of the life of the Abbey today. For just as the medieval Abbey was an integral part of the life of the community, so too the modern church touches that life at many points. Westminster Abbey is a splendid monument but not a museum. Its splendour is a living splendour still.

A DAY IN THE LIFE OF THE ABBEY

An Abbey day begins at about seven o'clock in the morning, when the cleaners take up their endless task of sweeping and washing, dusting and polishing. The first shift of vergers starts to prepare for the day's services, and the seamstress arrives in the Sacristy for her highly skilled craft of keeping the vestments, some of them 300 years old, in good repair. At eight the daily Eucharist is celebrated in one of the chapels; and visitors are already trickling in, taking their chance to see a little of the building in reasonable peace. By the time the Office of Matins has been sung or said this trickle has become a flood. From all over the world young and old pour in. Guides are lecturing in a dozen languages, and a tidal wave of sound fills the building. But on the stroke of ten the noise is hushed as over the loudspeaker system the voice of the priest on duty, speaking from the sixteenth-century pulpit in the Nave, asks the crowds to be silent for a few moments, and leads them in prayer. This happens every hour on the hour, for first and foremost this is a House of God.

At midday, perhaps, a visiting choir from abroad comes and sings for a short while by the Grave of the Unknown Warrior at the west end, while visitors stand around and listen. Then at 12.30 the Nave may be cleared for a lunch-hour talk or service or, on a great festival, for a sung Eucharist. After lunch the crowds build up again until, at the end of the afternoon, the choir and clergy process in to sing the evening Office, drawing day by day on the unique riches of English and European church music to the worship and praise of God. Later there may be an organ recital or a concert; and once a week there is an opportunity for students and others to study and photograph the architecture and monuments free of charge. Finally the Abbey falls quiet. The doors are locked, and only the watchmen break the silence of the great church until the cycle begins again the next morning.

But this is only the framework of a day. Into this may be slotted any number of other things. There are the many special services, reflecting every aspect of the life of Britain and the Commonwealth. Some of these come round every year. In October the Judges and other members of the legal profession arrive to dedicate their work at the beginning of another Michaelmas Law Term, hundreds of them, led by the Lord Chancellor, looking in their wigs and robes like a whole portrait gallery of history come to life. Another day it will be all the new graduates of the University of London for their Presentation Day service; on another, more than 2,000 nurses in uniform to commemorate Florence Nightingale. In June representatives of every country in the British Commonwealth assemble for the Commonwealth Observance, when not only Christian but Jewish, Muslim, Hindu and Buddhist religious leaders read from their scriptures, and all pray together for peace, justice and brotherhood among men. In September there is the national thanksgiving for deliverance in the Battle of Britain in 1940.

These are but a few striking examples from the Abbey's annual calendar. In addition there are the particular occasions: memorial services on the death of some notable figure in church or state; organisations celebrating some major anniversary. Charities, men and women of the armed forces, teachers, schools, senior citizens, civic leaders, artists, musicians, scientists, political parties – hardly any facet of national life is unrepresented. And every weekday during their school terms the boys of Westminster School come for their morning service. The Abbey is used for acts of worship, recollection and rededication for a higher proportion of each day than perhaps any other church in the world.

Then there are those events with which Westminster Abbey is especially associated in people's minds: royal occasions. For 900 years kings and queens of England have come here to be crowned – for 600 of those years in the same Coronation Chair (see p. 46) which Edward I had made to take the sacred Stone of Scone which he plundered from Scotland. In modern times many members of the Royal Family have been married here; and television coverage of such events has made the Abbey, inside and out, familiar to millions all over the world.

Finally, the Abbey's independence in church matters makes it a good meeting-place for the development of ecumenical co-operation and understanding. Not only do representatives of all the major churches in Britain attend the royal and special services, as one would expect on occasions concerning the nation as a whole or a cross-section of its citizens, but Sunday by Sunday members of many Christian denominations from all parts of the world are to be found worshipping here, communicating at the altar, and not infrequently preaching from the pulpit.

THE ABBEY AND ITS PRECINCTS

Most people perforce approach Westminster Abbey from the bustle of Parliament Square or Victoria Street; but let us begin in our mind's eye from the green seclusion of Dean's Yard (p. 9). Here the great west towers and the south face of the Nave, with the marvellously clean parallels of its flying buttresses, rise like a rampart keeping back the noise and rush of the world. In this area in medieval times were the almshouses, the monks' farm buildings and mill, and various apartments. In the north-east corner, nearest to the Abbey church, were the cellarer's hall and the sleeping quarters for the lay brothers.

Today the quietness masks even more activity. The south side of the Yard is formed by Church House, the administrative headquarters of the Church of England. On the east lie the Abbey's own offices and West-minster School. The latter, one of Britain's leading independent schools, traces its origin to the school run by the medieval monastery. After the dissolution of the monastery Henry VIII included in his new arrange-ments for the Abbey a King's Grammar School with two masters and forty scholars. This basic pattern was elaborated in the Charter granted by Elizabeth I, whom the School commemorates as in a very real sense its true Foundress. To this day there are forty 'Queen's Scholars' at West-minster, whose privilege it is to acclaim the Sovereign's entrance at a Coronation with shouts of 'Vivat!' from the Triforium. On the west of the Yard stands the Abbey's Choir School, while the rest of the buildings both here and on the north side are occupied by professional and business firms and private residents.

Looking up at the church itself, solidly reassuring by day, by night an even vaster mystery of patterned shadow and silver, one can still sense both the inspiration and the security which it must have brought to the Benedictine community of the Middle Ages, and which it still brings to the seven clergy and 120 or more lay men and women whose work keeps the Abbey and all its activities going today, and who like to think of themselves in an echo of the old monastic ideal as the 'Abbey Family'.

Leaving Dean's Yard and approaching the West Front of the church, it is easy to overlook, just behind the Abbey Bookshop, a castellated stone outbuilding with the slightly less pointed windows characteristic of English fourteenth-century Gothic. Yet this is one of the most historic rooms in England – the Jerusalem Chamber (p. 12). How it got its name is not known; possibly the original wall-hangings depicted the Holy

The south face of the Abbey, seen from Dean's Yard. Note the strong simplicity of the flying buttresses.

La façade sud de l'abbaye, vue de la cour du doyen. Remarquez la simplicité et la puissance des arcs-boutants.

Die Südfassade der Abtei vom Dean's Yard aus gesehen. Bemerkenswert ist die streng einfache Gestaltung der Strebebögen.

City. It was built in the late fourteenth century by Abbot Nicholas Littlington, whose monogram with that of his sovereign, Richard II (portrait, p. 19), decorates the original ceiling, rediscovered under a false one in the 1870s. The name of the room plays a dramatic part in its first appearance in history. In 1413 Henry IV visited the Shrine of the Confessor to prepare for a pilgrimage to the Holy Land which he planned to undertake in obedience to a prophecy that he would die 'in Jerusalem'. While praying he suffered a massive stroke. In the words of Fabyan's *Chronicles*, '. . . they for his comfort bore him into the Abbot's place and and laid him down before the fire in this chamber. On coming to himself and learning that he was in the chamber named Hierusalem, then said the king, "Laud be to the Father of Heaven! for now I know that I shall die in this chamber according to the prophecy . . .", and so he made himself ready and died shortly after.' The incident is referred to in Shakespeare's *Henry IV*, Part II, Act IV, Sc. 5.

But the Chamber's main claim to fame is that here in 1611 the Translators of the Authorised Version of the Bible (known in the United States as the King James Version) completed their labours. Of all the many renderings of the Bible into English this has been easily the most universally admired and influential. Phrases from it, often borrowed unconsciously, have for centuries decorated not only every kind of literature but also our common speech; and though advances in scholarship may mean that more recent translations gradually replace it for practical purposes, it will surely remain for all time, with the works of Shakespeare, a supreme monument of the English language. We should remember, however, that the Authorised Version was itself the distillation and refinement of a whole series of translations, reaching right back to Wycliffe in the fourteenth century; and the development of this tradition has gone on into modern times. So it was that, out of reverence for their predecessors, the Translators of the Revised Version of 1884 (the equivalent of the American Standard Version) also met here; and so did the main committee of those who produced one of the best known twentieth-century renderings, the New English Bible. For all English-speaking people who reverence the Christian Scriptures this is hallowed ground.

The overmantel in the Chamber was put in by Dean Williams in 1624 to celebrate the betrothal of Charles, Prince of Wales (later King Charles I), to Henrietta Maria of France, in the negotiations for which

The West Front. At the bottom right-hand corner is the Jerusalem Chamber. Private houses once stood along the north face.

La façade ouest. En bas et à droite, la Chambre de Jérusalem. Il y avait autrefois des maisons particulières le long de la façade nord.

Die Westfassade. In der unteren rechten Ecke ist die Jerusalem Chamber. Entlang der Nordfassade standen einst Wohnhäuser.

The Abbey from the north-west, showing the North Porch, in medieval times the royal entrance.

L'abbaye vue du nord-ouest, avec le portail nord qui était, au moyen-âge, l'entrée royale.

Blick von Nordwesten auf die Abtei mit dem Nordportal, im Mittelalter der Eingang für die Könige.

he had been much involved. There seems to have been quite a fashion at
the time for amateurs to portray this royal couple in, for example, stump-
work embroidery pieces, usually with unflattering results. Dean Williams's
carver introduced their heads three times into his design and, it must be
said, equally disastrously. The Dean also entertained the French Ambassador, Villoclare, to mark the engagement. There was Choral Evensong
in the Abbey, with all the choirmen wearing gorgeous copes; and Villoclare was presented with a specially bound copy of the Book of Common
Prayer translated into French. This was followed by a magnificent
banquet in the Chamber, which was then and still is officially part of the
Dean's domestic accommodation. But those were not ecumenically
minded days. The Ambassador kept his hat on in church, left his Prayer
book behind, and afterwards complained bitterly to the King about the
Dean's boring insistence on talking theology during dinner!

In 1642 the Long Parliament appointed a synod to reform the English
Church, and from the autumn of 1643 until 1649 this met in the Jerusalem
Chamber for a total of no fewer than 1,163 sessions. Its main achievements
were the Westminster Confession, the classic statement of Presbyterian
doctrine in the English-speaking world, and the Longer and Shorter

Catechisms, the latter being the one which begins with the famous question and answer: 'What is the chief end of Man? – Man's chief end is to glorify God and to enjoy Him for ever.' It is because of these associations that the word 'Westminster' appears in the names of Presbyterian colleges and institutions in many countries.

From 1689 to 1717 the Bishops of the Upper House of Convocation regularly met here, where there was a warm fire, while the lesser clergy shivered in Henry VII's Chapel. Not surprisingly there were some furious wrangles outside the Chamber in the Jericho Parlour (built by Abbot Islip in 1516 and containing superb linenfold panelling: see p. 13), when members of the Lower House came to make representations to the bishops. In 1725 the foreign ambassadors assembled here to robe before the first installation of knights in the reconstituted Order of the Bath; and during the first half of the eighteenth century several famous people lay in state in the Chamber before burial in the Abbey, notably Sir Isaac Newton.

Today the Chamber is in constant use for the conduct of Abbey business by the Dean and Chapter, and for the entertainment of guests, and also by numerous outside bodies. It is instructive to reflect that in 1837 a 'Report for the Improvement of the Metropolis' seriously suggested that the Chamber be pulled down. The planners, it would seem, have been always with us.

The advice often given to visitors to the Abbey is, 'Keep your eyes up!' Certainly, if one becomes too engrossed in the innumerable monuments, one does miss the essential glory of the building, the sweep, line and proportion of the uniquely unified architectural design. The secret of the

East Cloister. Door of the Pyx Chamber, once a royal treasury. Chapter House porch beyond.

Le cloître est. La porte de la Chambre de Pyx, qui faisait autrefois partie du trésor royal. Plus loin, le porche du Chapître.

Der Ostkreuzgang. Die Tür zur Pyx Chamber, einst eine königliche Schatzkammer. Dahinter das Portal des Chapter House.

Modern restoration in the South Cloister by Abbey masons shows that ancient skills live on.

Les restaurations modernes effectuées dans le cloître sud par des maçons de l'abbaye montrent que les métiers anciens survivent.

Moderne Renovierungsarbeiten im Südkreuzgang durch Steinmetze der Abtei beweisen, dass alte Fertigkeiten noch nicht ausgestorben sind.

church's special aesthetic appeal is that it is a perfect marriage of English and French Gothic: the inspiration is French, the execution and detail purely English. Henry III's architect, Master Henry of Reynes, who may have been a Frenchman, though this is not certain, completed the new church from the Apse as far westward as the Choir Screen between the years 1245 and 1272.

The work is marked by many touches of genius. The proportions of the Choir (continued in the Nave), which combine an interior height of 103 feet with a width of only 35 feet, a ratio of virtually 3 to 1, give the sublime soaring effect characteristic of French Gothic without the technical problems created by structures as tall, for example, as Beauvais. The

BENEATH THIS STONE RESTS THE B
OF A BRITISH WARRIOR
UNKNOWN BY NAME OR RANK
BROUGHT FROM FRANCE TO LIE AMONG
THE MOST ILLUSTRIOUS OF THE LAND
AND BURIED HERE ON ARMISTICE DAY
11 NOV: 1920, IN THE PRESENCE OF
HIS MAJESTY KING GEORGE V
HIS MINISTERS OF STATE
THE CHIEFS OF HIS FORCES
AND A VAST CONCOURSE OF THE NATION
THUS ARE COMMEMORATED THE MANY
MULTITUDES WHO DURING THE GREAT
WAR OF 1914-1918 GAVE THE MOST THAT
MAN CAN GIVE LIFE ITSELF
FOR GOD
FOR KING AND COUNTRY
FOR LOVED ONES HOME AND EMPIRE
FOR THE SACRED CAUSE OF JUSTICE AND
THE FREEDOM OF THE WORLD
THEY BURIED HIM AMONG THE KINGS BECAUSE HE
HAD DONE GOOD TOWARD GOD AND TOWARD
HIS HOUSE

sharply pointed arches, again typical of early French Gothic, remind one in their joyful freshness of newly thrusting leaves in spring (for the same effect in the Nave aisles, see p. 21). One of the most subtle features is the design of the Apse. The plan called for a rounded east end, incorporating a series of apsidal chapels to encircle the focal sacred point, the Shrine of the Confessor. But the proportion of width to height just described meant that no more than three facets of one arch apiece could be used to complete the semicircle, an arrangement liable to give a crude and jerky effect. The problem was solved by the ingenious device of angling the last bay of each side wall inwards a few degrees only, so little that it is easy not to notice the fact unless one's attention is drawn to it, but enough to give a smooth flow to the three bays of the end wall. (This feature can just be detected in the picture on p. 16).

Equally remarkable, however, and a factor which has contributed just as much to the very special impact of the Abbey interior was the decision of Master Henry Yevele, the architect in charge when work on the Nave recommenced in 1377, not to use a design of his own but to continue

The Grave of the Unknown Warrior (west end of Nave).

La tombe du Guerrier Inconnu (extrémité ouest de la nef).

Das Grab des Unbekannten Soldaten im Westende der Kirche.

Richard II, devotee of the Confessor (west end of Nave).

Richard II, dévoué à Edouard le Confesseur (extrémité ouest de la nef).

Richard II., Verehrer des Bekenners (Westende des Kirchenschiffes).

that of his great predecessor. As the sequence of changing styles in many churches and cathedrals shows, such a decision must have required both originality and strength of mind. Yevele's successors followed his example; and though the work proceeded only in short bursts as money became available (Henry V was a generous benefactor) and was not finally completed until 1502 under Abbot Islip, the result is that when we look down the whole length of the main church today we have the sense of a single magnificent conception brought to near-perfect expression (see p. 17).

What did change as the work went on was, of course, the details of mouldings and carving, which were left to the masons of each generation to do in the taste of their own day; but this variety adds to the richness of the whole, because it is integrated into the strong overall design. One slight impoverishment, presumably for reasons of cost, is that the roof bosses in the Nave are smaller and less ornate than those in the Choir; but they are still fully worthy of the whole. The same cannot always be said of later ingredients, in particular of the Choir Screen (p. 16), which was the work of Edward Blore. Blore was Surveyor of the Fabric (the title given to the architect retained by the Dean and Chapter to care for the building) in the thirties and forties of the nineteenth century. He was responsible for the present arrangement of the Choir and Transepts. The latter had previously been screened off, but Blore opened them up and made them available for congregational use, an immense improvement without which modern worship in the Abbey could hardly have developed. He also re-designed the Choir, the present choir stalls in the Victorian Gothic manner (p. 25) being his work. These have stood the test of time, but it may be doubted whether the same can be said for the west face of the Screen.

Nevertheless the Screen itself is a remarkable structure, having the organ loft on top of it. The visitor who passes through from Nave to Choir probably never realises how large this loft is. In addition to the organ console there is room for the full choir, a small orchestra and a fanfare of trumpets – an invaluable facility on great ceremonial occasions. One tricky technical problem is that of co-ordinating the music precisely with points in a service, such as the start of a procession, which may take place out of sight of the organist or conductor on the Screen. In the past this was done by hand signals or telephonic communication. Now, however, there is a closed circuit television system (the gift of the First National Bank of Boston, USA) which enables the organist to see exactly what is happening in the Henry VII Chapel and at the Great West Door, and to watch the beat given by whoever is conducting the Choir below.

The office of Surveyor has in its time been held by many eminent architects. The most famous by far was Sir Christopher Wren, who devoted his genius and enthusiasm unstintingly to the Abbey's preservation and improvement from 1698 until his death in 1723. Other well-known names include Benjamin Wyatt, Sir Gilbert Scott and J. L. Pearson. To the interior Scott contributed the fine Reredos to the High Altar (p. 26)

This view of the South Nave Aisle shows the sharp, leaf-like vaulting typical of French Gothic style in the springtime of the Middle Ages.

Cette vue du bas-côté sud de la nef montre la voûte précise et aérienne typique du style gothique français en vogue au début du moyen-âge.

Dieser Blick in das südliche Seitenschiff zeigt den scharfen, blattähnlichen Gewölbestyle der französischen Gotik im frühen Mittelalter.

and Pearson the organ cases (p. 25), while the North Transept Front embodies the work of both.

Designing furnishings to blend with an ancient building of such decided character is never easy. One distinguished modern example is that of the sixteen chandeliers of Waterford glass which hang in the Nave and the Transepts (see, e.g., p. 17), and which were a gift to the Abbey from the Guinness family to mark the 900th anniversary year. Each chandelier is ten feet in length (a fact which gives one a useful indication of scale when looking upwards), weighs 280 lb. (127 kilos), and contains 539 separate pieces of crystal.

Just inside the Great West Door is a memorial which is a hallowed place of pilgrimage to many thousands and of memories for tens of thousands more: the Grave of the Unknown Warrior (p. 18). Here on Armistice Day, 11 November 1920, was buried the body of an unknown British soldier to represent the supreme sacrifice made by 1,069,825 of his fellow-citizens from the United Kingdom and the Commonwealth during the First World War. Every year on Remembrance Sunday heads of the three Armed Forces lead a packed congregation in paying silent

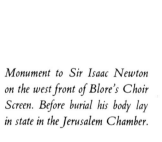

Monument to Sir Isaac Newton on the west front of Blore's Choir Screen. Before burial his body lay in state in the Jerusalem Chamber.

Le monument à Sir Isaac Newton sur la façade ouest du paravent d'Edouard Blore dans le chœur. Avant son enterrement, son corps fut exposé dans la Chambre de Jérusalem.

Denkmal für Sir Isaac Newton an der Westseite von Blores Chor-schranke. Vor der Bestattung war sein Leichnam in der Jerusalem Chamber aufgebahrt.

homage at this spot, a commemoration which today, of course, includes all those who died in the Second World War and in subsequent conflicts in which British forces were engaged, such as Korea. But this is far from the only occasion on which such remembrance is made here. Every foreign Head of State on a State Visit to this country comes here soon after his arrival to lay a wreath; and foreign diplomats, crews of naval vessels visiting London, and a host of Servicemen's organisations, of all nationalities, do the same, not to mention private individuals.

But beyond its message of heroism in defence of liberty and country the Grave also says something about all the memorials in this Abbey church. The quotation from the Bible at the foot of the inscription reads: 'They buried him among the kings because he had done good toward God and toward his house'; and this applies to the great majority of those who have found burial here. Fourteen kings and fifteen queens rest within these walls, but also almost 3,000 of their subjects. Of these some are among the most famous in their country's history, but of others the names now mean little or nothing. Sometimes people ask, 'Why was he buried here, I wonder?' The answer is simply that their contemporaries thought that these men or women had done good. Their work or fame was not necessarily of the kind that history later judges to have been of lasting importance; but it mattered to their fellow-citizens to honour them.

Because of this the monuments in the Abbey have lessons of abiding value to teach us. They speak of values which our forebears held dear, and which we may from time to time forget and need to recover: the courage and integrity of lawyers and public servants; the uncynical ideals of the young; the devotion to study and education of doctors and obscure schoolmasters and experts in the by-ways of knowledge; the piety and fervour of religious souls; the loyalty of those who were simply good friends and faithful members of society, kind and courteous and generous to the poor. The fact that such as these find their place alongside the rulers and the great is an eloquent witness to the true nature of the good society and the importance of every individual within it. For this reason it is to be regretted that no Sovereign since George II has been buried in the Abbey. An important part of the symbolism has been lost.

The decision as to whether or not burial in the Abbey should be given to any particular individual rests, except where the Sovereign is involved, with the Dean. (A high-ranking Soviet official whom the author once showed round the Abbey was plainly sceptical about this – such decisions must be the prerogative of the Government!) For a long time it has also been the practice to memorialise some who are in fact buried elsewhere. Not all the slabs in the floor mark the graves of those whose names they bear. But as you go round the Abbey you will often come across a wreath or a simple bunch of flowers laid on tomb or memorial, left there as a silent and anonymous testimony of affection and respect by someone who has slipped in for a few moments and gone their way unnoticed. Even the monuments should not be thought of merely as dead records. They still have a living meaning.

The Nave commemorates an extraordinary variety of famous people. Immediately inside the West Door a green marble slab reads, 'Remember Winston Churchill', just a few paces from a wall plaque in honour of Franklin D. Roosevelt, President of the United States. In the north-west corner are clustered leaders of the Radical tradition in British life, and near them philanthropists such as Lord Shaftesbury and the American, George Peabody, who did so much for the London poor. In the north-east corner is St George's Chapel, primarily dedicated to the military, but also remembering such spiritual fighters as William Booth, founder of the Salvation Army, and Charles Kingsley. This Chapel is now set aside for private prayer. Just to the east of it Lord Baden-Powell is memorialised; his grave is at Nyeri in Kenya.

In place of honour in the centre aisle of the Nave lies David Livingstone, the undaunted missionary, explorer and champion of the rights of the native African. Hard by are Thomas Tompion, the world-famous clockmaker, and Thomas Telford, the road- and bridge-builder, a pioneer of modern engineering technology fitly marked by a recent inscription using a new technique of brass inlaid in cast iron which, it is expected, will last many generations longer than the conventional method of brass in marble. Toward the Screen, near the monument of Sir Isaac Newton (p. 23), lie the physicists Faraday and Clerk Maxwell, the astronomer Herschel, and – a surprise to many visitors – Charles Darwin. In his lifetime Darwin's writings sparked off that conflict between science and religion the consequences of which are with us still. But today most Christians recognise that this was a sad and unnecessary battle, and are glad that one of the intellectual giants who laid the foundation of our modern understanding of the world should lie here in the house of the

Previous page: The Choir, where the monks sang the Offices. The stalls (1848) are the work of Edward Blore, the organ cases that of Pearson.

Page précédente: Le chœur, où les moines chantaient les offices. Les stalles datant de 1848 sont l'œuvre d'Edouard Blore et les coffrages de l'orgue sont de Pearson.

Vorgehende Seite: Der Chor, in dem Mönche die Offizien sangen. Das Gestühl ist von Edward Blore, die Orgelrahmen von Pearson.

One of the silver-gilt seventeenth-century candlesticks on the High Altar, the gift of Sarah Hughes. Behind is part of a festal dorsal given by King George V and Queen Mary.

Ce chandelier en argent doré du dix-septième siècle, qui se trouve sur le maître-autel, est l'un de ceux offerts par Sarah Hughes. On peut voir derrière une partie d'une parure d'autel offerte par le roi Georges V et la reine Marie.

Einer der vergoldeten Silberleuchter aus dem 17. Jahrhundert auf dem Hochaltar, das Geschenk von Sarah Hughes. Dahinter ist ein Teil des von König George V. und Königin Mary gestifteten festlichen Dorsals.

The Sanctuary and High Altar. On the left is the great Cross of Westminster. The Cosmati floor, once the finest in the world, is now too ruinous to be uncovered.

Le sanctuaire et le maître-autel. Sur la gauche, la grande croix de Westminster. Le sol de Cosmati, qui fut le plus beau au monde, est maintenant trop abîmé pour être découvert.

Der Altarplatz mit dem Hochaltar. Links das grosse Kreuz von Westminster. Der Fussboden von Cosmati, einst der schönste in der Welt, ist überdeckt, um ihn vor weiterem Schaden zu bewahren.

In the North Transept the great
of this world stand under the Rose
Window (1722) portraying those
great in heaven.

Dans le transept nord les grands
de ce monde se tiennent sous la
rosace (de 1722) qui représente
ceux qui sont grands dans les cieux.

Im Nordquerschiff stehen die
Grossen dieser Welt unter den
Grossen im Himmel im Rosetten-
fenster (1722).

God in whom he himself could not believe but whom we know so
much better as a result of his discoveries.

The North Choir Aisle is devoted chiefly to musicians; and here it
may be appropriate to say something about the place of music in the life
of the Abbey. In the sixteenth century England was one of the leading
musical nations of Europe, and men like Gibbons, Tallis and Byrd
created a body of works in the polyphonic style which rank with those of
continental composers such as Lassus, Palestrina and Victoria. Today
these works are increasingly performed on the concert platform; but for
some 300 years they survived almost exclusively in the repertoire of
churches like Westminster Abbey and cathedrals and college chapels.
This tradition called for high standards of musicianship which were not
always maintained; the period between 1750 and 1850 was especially

marked by periods of slackness and incompetence. Nevertheless the Abbey has had its fair share of distinguished names among its organists, pre-eminent being Orlando Gibbons (1623–5) and Henry Purcell (1679–95), two of the greatest composers these islands have produced. In recent times Sir Sydney Nicholson (1919–28) was founder of the Royal School of Church Music.

The practice of having singing boys in the choir goes back to monastic times. In 1479 William Cornyshe was appointed 'Master of the Song Scole', and about the same time the Abbey was given the right to conscript good singers from other choirs. The golden age of Elizabethan and Jacobean music was succeeded by a brief but dismal period under the Commonwealth when the musical establishment was suppressed. John Vicars, a Puritan writer of the time, comments on the change with intense satisfaction: '. . . whereas there was wont to be heard nothing almost but roaring boys and squeaking organ pipes, and the cathedral catches of Morley, and I know not what trash; now . . . the bellowing organs are demolisht, . . . the treble, or rather trouble and base singers, chanters or inchanters driven out; and instead thereof, . . . every morning throughout the weeke, and every weeke through the whole yeare a sermon is preached . . .' Fortunately the Restoration came to the rescue. Today the choristers are drawn from thirty-six boys educated residentially in the Abbey Choir School. The men singers of the Abbey choir, known as Lay Vicars, also have a long history, closely linked with that of the Gentlemen of the Chapel Royal. Nowadays many of them are well-known professional soloists; and the resultant high standards are reflected in the performance of the boys, who themselves frequently go on to musical careers.

The Abbey has made other contributions to the nation's musical life. In 1784 was held the great Handel Commemoration, when audiences of almost 3,000 gathered to hear two concerts given by a choir of 275 and an orchestra of 249 players, massed on huge stands built up against the west end wall of the Nave. So successful were these that similar festivals were held in the next three years, and again in 1791, on which occasion no less a person than Haydn was present. These concerts were of major significance, since they started the tradition of large choral societies and music festivals which have come to mean so much in our culture. In 1871 the Abbey was the scene of another great musical event – the first church performance in England of Bach's St Matthew Passion, which again went on to establish itself everywhere as a deeply loved work. In 1962 Britten's War Requiem received its London première in the Abbey; and concerts have now become a regular feature of Abbey life. The Westminster Abbey Special Choir, with several hundred members drawn from churches all over the London area, gives recitals two or three times a year, and helps to spread the ideal of good musicianship ever more widely.

In the North Choir Aisle lie Gibbons, Purcell, Stanford, Blow and Vaughan Williams, and Elgar and Britten are commemorated.

During the Second World War the Abbey was fortunate enough to

The South Transept. The glass (1902) in the Rose Window depicts the Preparation and Preaching of the Gospel. Note the carvings of the two censing angels at the bottom corners.

Le transept sud. Dans la rosace, le vitrail (datant de 1902) décrit la préparation et la propagation de l'évangile. Remarquez les deux anges encenseurs sculptés dans les coins du bas.

Das Südquerschiff. Die Glasmalerei (1902) im Rosettenfenster stellt die Ankündigung und das Predigen des Evangeliums dar. Man beachte der beiden beweihräuchernden Engel in den unteren Ecken.

suffer only one major damage, the destruction of the roof of the Lantern as a result of a fire started by an incendiary bomb. Though the roof fell to the floor of the crossing, 130 feet below, it luckily did no serious harm inside the church; and the replacement is altogether finer than what preceded it, which was only a 'temporary' affair, dating from around 1800! The large open space under the Lantern is important for two reasons. One is that it contributes materially to the majesty of this part of the church; the other, that it provides an incomparable arena for great ceremonies. This is the spot where, at coronations, the stage is erected on which the Sovereign receives the homage of the Lords Spiritual and Temporal. The fine black and white pavement of the Lantern and Choir was the gift of Dr Richard Busby (1606–95), a celebrated Head Master of Westminster School, who is buried beneath it.

Standing in the Lantern we can study the High Altar and Scott's Reredos (p. 26). On this altar are two witnesses to one of the most touching human stories in the Abbey's history, the two silver gilt candlesticks (p. 27). These were the gift of Sarah Hughes, who in the seventeenth century was a serving maid at Westminster School. All her long life she saved from her small wages, and at her death bequeathed a considerable sum to the Abbey. With great imagination the Dean and Chapter spent the money on something which would occupy the place of honour such sacrificial devotion deserved. When they first appeared on the altar, they would in the manner of the time have been the principal ornaments upon it. The cross is a later piece, the base of which was made to match that of Sarah's candlesticks.

To the right of the High Altar are the ancient sedilia. Of the medieval paintings which decorated the back panels two, perhaps representing King Edward I and King Henry III, have been successfully restored (for one, see p. 38), and are notable for their strong flowing line and rich colour.

Under the carpeting of the sanctuary are the remains of a unique treasure. In Henry III's reign Abbot Ware had to visit Rome to have his appointment confirmed by the Pope. There he was deeply impressed by the beauty of a method of decoration, called Cosmati work after the family which invented it, which consists of intricate designs in small pieces of coloured and polished marble set in a plain marble ground; and he brought back materials and skilled craftsmen to adorn the new Abbey church in this way. The King approved, and so Westminster became the only building outside Italy to possess Cosmati work. Two pavements, that before the High Altar and that of the Confessor's Shrine, were both decorated in this style, the former, its mystical design symbolising the age of the universe, being the most highly wrought Cosmati floor in the world. Sadly, however, soft Purbeck marble was used for the ground of the design instead of hard Italian white marble. Even in the eighteenth century the total pattern was still reasonably clear; but it later wore away so badly that virtually nothing of the original glory now remains, and both floors have to be kept covered to protect what is left. Some small idea

This fine, medieval wall-painting in the South Transept, to the left of the door of St Faith's Chapel, depicts the Risen Christ showing his side to Doubting Thomas.

Cette belle peinture murale du moyen-âge dans le transept sud, à gauche de la porte de la chapelle St Faith, représente le Christ ressuscité montrant son flanc à St Thomas.

Dieses feine mittelalterliche Wandgemälde im Südquerschiff, links von der Tür zur St.-Faith-Kapelle, stellt den auferstandenen Christus dar, wie er dem zweifelnden Thomas seine Wunden zeigt.

KEATS
1795-1821

SHELLEY
1792-1822

BURNS

ROBERT SOUTHEY.
BORN AUGUST 12TH 1774. DIED MARCH 21ST 1843.

JOHNSON

JAMES THOMSON

THOMAS CAMPBELL
BORN JULY XXVII. MDCCLXXVII.
DIED JUNE XV. MDCCCXLIV.

THIS SPIRIT SHALL RETURN TO HIM
WHO GAVE ITS HEAVENLY SPARK
YET THINK NOT, SUN, IT SHALL BE DIM
WHEN THOU THYSELF ART DARK
NO! IT SHALL LIVE AGAIN AND SHINE
IN BLISS UNKNOWN TO BEAMS OF THINE
BY HIM RECALL'D TO BREATH
WHO CAPTIVE LED CAPTIVITY
WHO ROBB'D THE GRAVE OF VICTORY
AND TOOK THE STING FROM DEATH

The 'Shakespeare Wall' in Poets' Corner (South Transept). The statue (1740) is sentimentally idealised; Horace Walpole called it 'preposterous'. Plaques commemorating other great poets have been added later.

Le « mur de Shakespeare » dans le Coin des Poètes (transept sud). La statue (de 1740) est sentimentale et idéalisée; Horace Walpole la trouvait « absurde ». Les plaques commémorant d'autres grands poètes ont été ajoutées plus tard.

Die „Shakespeare-Mauer" in Poets' Corner (Südquerschiff). Die Statue ist auf sentimentale Weise idealisiert; Horace Walpole bezeichnete sie als „widersinnig". Ehrentafeln für andere grosse Dichter sind später hinzugefügt worden.

In Poets' Corner, Epstein's bronze head of William Blake (1957), the finest modern work of art in the Abbey.

Dans le Coin des Poètes, la tête en bronze de William Blake par Epstein, exécutée en 1957, est la meilleure œuvre d'art moderne de l'abbaye.

Epsteins Bronzebüste von William Blake (1957) in der „Poetenecke" ist das beste moderne Kunstwerk in der Abtei.

of the richness of Cosmati decoration can be had from surviving elements of it on the tomb of Henry III (p. 47).

To north and south of the Lantern run the two transepts. The North Transept (see pp. 28–9) is best known for the imposing array in its east aisle of statues of great British statesmen: Castlereagh, Canning, Peel, Palmerston, Disraeli and Gladstone. In the west aisle are some of the most massive monuments in the Abbey; and even when they are artistically fine, or in honour of such men as William Pitt the Elder and Lord Mansfield, the Scotsman who was one of the greatest of all British lawyers, one can only regret that they render such large areas of the church unusable.

The South Transept is one of the most eagerly visited parts of the whole church, for here is the celebrated Poets' Corner, originally only the east aisle but now extending along the south wall as well. In 1400 Geoffrey Chaucer, the 'father of English poetry', was buried here, not however because he was a poet but as a senior official of the Royal Household. It was the burial in 1599 of Edmund Spenser, 'the Prince of Poets in his tyme', some feet to the south of Chaucer, which really began the custom of dedicating this part of the Abbey to poetry, Chaucer's own burial here being a fortuitous extra distinction. Among the more famous of those whose bodies actually lie here are Ben Jonson, Dryden, Tennyson, Browning and Masefield; but in this corner more than anywhere else the practice has established itself of seeking to memorialise all the most eminent in a particular sphere. Sometimes this has been done quickly in

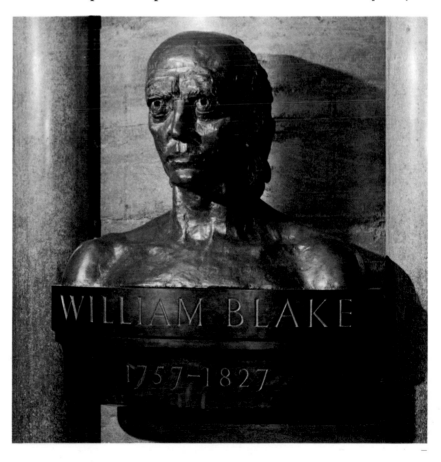

response to contemporary taste, sometimes long after the poet's death in the light of the verdict of history, and sometimes, as in the case of Shakespeare (p. 34), to fill an obvious gap in the collection. Milton, Longfellow, Wordsworth, Gray, Keats, Shelley, Burns, Byron, Blake, T. S. Eliot and Gerard Manley Hopkins are among the chief names in this category. Whether the practice is a good one is disputable. It compounds the overcrowding, and by giving the impression that a poet is not in the first rank until commemorated here it encourages literary lobbying. It may also be thought to detract from interest, which should instead be encouraged, in lesser known places where these great figures are actually buried.

Of other writers, Dr Johnson, Dickens, Thackeray, Sheridan, Kipling and Hardy are buried in the south-west section of the Transept, as is the composer Handel, whose statue is a striking feature of the west wall. Jane Austen, Goldsmith, Scott, Ruskin, the Brontës and Henry James are among those memorialised.

The mass of statuary in these two Transepts reminds one that for those interested in sculpture the Abbey affords an opportunity to study the work of many famous names, such as Grinling Gibbons, Nollekens, Roubiliac, Flaxman, Chantrey, and, of modern artists, Epstein, whose bronze head of Blake (p. 35) was placed here in 1957 to mark the bicentenary of the poet's birth.

But the South Transept is much more than a mausoleum for great men of letters. It is also an architectural glory (see p. 31). The south wall is one of the finest compositions in stone in any Gothic church in the world. The arches – five in the arcading at ground level, six in each of the two middle stages, and six windows grouped in three bold units at the top – are markedly but subtly different in each tier, cohering in a most satisfying manner with each other yet leading the eye effortlessly upward to the glorious Rose Window, at the bottom corners of which are the celebrated carvings of the censing angels, rightly regarded as 'supreme examples of English medieval art'. Also very fine are the two medieval wall-paintings, dating from 1280 to 1300, and depicting St Christopher and the Incredulity of St Thomas (p. 33).

A door in the same wall leads into St Faith's Chapel (see p. 37), which since 1898 has been reserved for private prayer. The early wall-paintings behind the altar have a primitive beauty. The main figure is that of St Faith herself. To the left a Benedictine monk kneels in prayer. At altar level there is also a small painting of the Passion. In the Middle Ages the Chapel was used as a vestry. It later became a storeroom, and remained so even after Sir Gilbert Scott had refurbished it. Finally, at the urging of Canon (later Bishop) Charles Gore, it was decided to use it for worship, in particular for weekday Eucharists; and today it is an oasis of peace and one of the best-loved corners of the Abbey.

One of the loveliest moments to be had in the whole church is a walk along the South Ambulatory on an early summer morning (p. 43), with the sunshine falling gently through the windows and the honey-coloured

Once a lumber-room, St Faith's Chapel has since 1898 been reserved wholly for worship and private devotion. In the medieval wall-painting a monk begs the Saint's prayers.

La Chapelle St Faith, qui fut à un moment donné utilisée comme débarras, est depuis 1898 entièrement réservée à la prière et à la dévotion. Dans cette peinture murale du moyen-âge, un moine supplie la sainte d'exaucer ses prières.

Die St.-Faith-Kapelle, einst eine Rumpelkammer, wird seit 1898 für Gottesdienste und private Andachten benutzt. In dem mittelalterlichen Wandgemälde bittet ein Mönch die Heilige um Fürsprachegebete.

Tomb of Gabriel Goodman (Dean 1571–1601) in the Chapel of St Benedict (South Transept). A great benefactor to education, he founded Christ's Hospital and Ruthin Grammar School.

La tombe de Gabriel Goodman (Doyen de 1571 à 1601) dans la Chapelle de St Benoît (St Benedict) (transept sud). Bienfaiteur de l'éducation, il fonda deux écoles: Christ's Hospital et Ruthin Grammar School.

Das Grabmal von Gabriel Goodman (Dekan 1571–1601) in der St.-Benedict-Kapelle (Südquerschiff). Als grosser Förderer der Erziehung gründete er Christ's Hospital und Ruthin Grammar School.

Medieval painting from the sedilia to the south of the High Altar, probably portraying King Henry III. The solidity of the figure is remarkable for the period.

Cette peinture médiévale sur la sedia au sud du maître-autel représente probablement le roi Henri III. La solidité de la silhouette est remarquable pour l'époque.

Das mittelalterliche Gemälde von der Sedilie südlich des Hochaltars stellt wahrscheinlich König Henry III. dar. Die Festigkeit der Figur ist bemerkenswert für die Epoche.

stone screen of St. Nicholas's Chapel to lie in magical golden pools on the floor, and the gentle curve of the building beckoning one on, suggesting new mysteries of peace and sanctity beyond. The chapels both here and in the North Ambulatory are no longer usable, alas, for worship as they would have been in the Middle Ages when the priests of the community said Mass in them day by day. They are completely filled with monuments commemorating various noble and wealthy citizens of the sixteenth and seventeenth centuries. These brilliantly painted memorials (see, e.g. p. 44), rich with portrait statuary and *trompe-l'oeil* work, have been restored in recent years to their original magnificence. But though they are of great interest and charm in themselves, one cannot help sensing a note of arrogance and self-satisfaction, a product perhaps of the vitality and expansionism of the period, when one compares them with the more restrained and discreet graves of various medieval abbots and minor royalty also to be found in this part of the church. In the Ambulatory itself, at the eastern end, is a thirteenth-century Retable, which must once have stood behind one of the altars removed at the Reformation. This is now much damaged, but enough remains to show what its beauty must once have been. At the left-hand end of the bottom border is one tiny surviving cameo, perhaps the oldest-known medieval example of this delicate art.

At the beginning of the North Ambulatory is the little Islip Chapel (see p. 50), a spot with a lovely atmosphere of meditative seclusion. John Islip was the last great builder of the medieval abbots; he finished the Nave and constructed the lower half of the two western towers. The

Simon Langham, Abbot, Archbishop of Canterbury, Lord Chancellor, Cardinal, and munificent benefactor of the Abbey, lies in St Benedict's Chapel.

Islip Chapel is dedicated to the Holy Name of Jesus, and is one of the side chapels in which the Eucharist is still celebrated weekly. Above it is a chantry chapel where Masses were once said for the Abbot's soul, and which is now a Nurses' Memorial Chapel in which are recorded the names of nurses and midwives who died during the Second World War. It is a sad commentary on our times that one can now be admitted to these chapels only if accompanied by a verger, since the upper chapel has so often been damaged and desecrated by visitors allowed into it on their own.

At the top of a double flight of steps leading out of the Ambulatory and behind two splendid gates made of bronze on wood is the Chapel of Our Lady, known universally as the Henry VII Chapel. This building is one of those works of art – there are not many in the whole world – which simply defeat any effort to catch their visual beauty in language. Few indeed of the one and a half million people who pass through it each year fail to be stirred, even shaken by its perfection. But you do not hear them say much as they lift their eyes to take in the wonder of it all – just a trite exclamation, perhaps, and then they are content to look.

The South Ambulatory, showing St Nicholas's Chapel and Edward III's tomb (close-up, facing page).

La Chapelle St Nicholas et la tombe d'Edouard III (en face).

Der südliche Wandelgang mit der St.-Nicholas-Kapelle und dem Grab Edwards III. (gegenüber).

The opulent self-confidence of the
Elizabethan and Jacobean periods
lives on in these gorgeously carved
and coloured monuments in St
Nicholas's Chapel.

*La sérénité opulente des époques
Elisabéthaine et Jacobéenne survit
avec ces monuments magnifique-
ment sculptés et colorés de la
Chapelle St Nicholas.*

*In diesen reich geformten und
bemalten Skulpturen in der St.-
Nicholas-Kapelle spiegelt sich das
grosse Selbstvertrauen der elisa-
bethanischen und jakobischen
Epochen.*

The Confessor's Shrine. Its
present form dates from 1557 when
the Shrine, dismantled at the
Reformation, was partially (and
incorrectly) restored. Traces of
original enamelling survive on the
twisted pillars.

*La châsse d'Edouard le Confes-
seur. Sa forme contemporaine date
de 1557, lorsque la châsse fut
partiellement (et incorrectement)
restaurée après avoir été démantelée
à l'époque de la Réforme. Des
traces de l'émail d'origine sont
encore visibles sur les piliers
torsadés.*

*Der Schrein des Bekenners. In
heutiger Gestalt stammt er aus dem
Jahre 1557, als der Schrein, nach
Entfernung während der Reformation, teilweise (und unrichtig)
wiedererrichtet wurde. Spuren der
ursprünglichen Emaillearbeiten
überleben an den Pfeilern.*

Which is just as it should be. In this book, fortunately, we have the pic-
tures (see pp. 53, 56-7) to make the search for adjectives and imagery
unnecessary. A little information, however, may be of interest.

The architect of the Chapel was Robert Vertue, one of Henry VII's
master masons. He had one important advantage on his side – his brother,
William Vertue, had recently (1505) designed and built the roof of St
George's Chapel, Windsor, which with this Chapel and that of King's
College, Cambridge, makes up the trio of supreme masterpieces in the
English Perpendicular style. The Henry VII Chapel is the latest of the
three (the foundation stone was laid by Islip in 1503, and the whole
finished in 1519-20), and the builders undoubtedly profited from the
ideas and mistakes of these earlier buildings to come even closer to their
ideal.

As we would expect in the circumstances, the Chapel is highly unified
and integrated in conception and execution. In this respect it is like the
main Abbey church; and because of the gradual approach to it by way
of the Ambulatory and up the staircase and then through the boundary-

44

mark of the bronze gates, which are densely enough textured to be a
real barrier but so pierced as to intimate that beyond them lies a new world
whose character is already hinted at in their own distinctive design, we
do not feel any clash or conflict between their very different glories. One

The Chapel of the Holy Name of Jesus, created by Abbot John Islip (1464–1532), the 'great builder', who lies buried in this place of prayerful peace.

La chapelle du Saint Nom de Jésus, créée par l'abbé John Islip (1464–1532), dit le « grand bâtisseur », qui repose dans ce lieu de paix et de prière.

Die Chapel of the Holy Name of Jesus wurde erbaut von Abt John Islip (1464–1532), dem „grossen Baumeister", der an diesem heiligen Ort des Friedens begraben liegt.

plates recording the names and arms of past knights. Notable too are the carved misericordes, which survive from the monastic use of the Chapel.

At the east end, behind the altar with its Virgin and Child by Vivarini (p. 58), is Henry VII's great bronze tomb (p. 59), the work of the Florentine master, Pietro Torrigiano. The easternmost apsidal chapel is now the Royal Air Force Chapel (p. 63), and has a fine modern window by Hugh Easton in memory of those of 'the Few' killed in the Battle of Britain.

In the North Aisle two queens, both daughters of Henry VIII, the Catholic Mary I and the Protestant Elizabeth I, each guilty of persecuting the other side during the Reformation struggles, share a common tomb. In the floor nearby a marble slab has now been laid, bearing these words in red on white: 'Near the tomb of Mary and Elizabeth remember before God all those who, divided at the Reformation by convictions sincerely held, laid down their lives for Christ and conscience sake.' May this do something to bring healing today where these same divisions, further poisoned by ideological hatred, have bred so much violence and misery!

Returning westward from the Henry VII Chapel, we cross a bridge given to the Abbey by the Institute of Civil Engineers, pass the tomb of Henry V, and enter the heart of the whole building, the original reason for its very existence, the Chapel which contains what is left of the Shrine

St John the Baptist Chapel. Thomas Cecil, Earl of Exeter, and his wife lie before the tomb of Henry Carey, Baron Hunsdon, an overwhelming example of Elizabethan monumental art.

La chapelle de St Jean Baptiste. Thomas Cecil, Comte d'Exeter, et sa femme, reposent devant la tombe d'Henry Carey, le baron Hunsdon. Cette tombe est un exemple magistral de l'art monumental de l'époque Elisabéthaine.

St. John the Baptist Chapel. Thomas Cecil, Earl of Exeter, und seine Gemahlin ruhen vor dem Grabmal von Henry Carey, Baron Hunsdon, ein überzeugendes Beispiel für die elisabethanische Monumentalkunst.

of Edward the Confessor (see p. 45). It is not easy in a dense and jostling crowd to re-create today the numinous atmosphere which once invested this place, the focus of the fervent devotion of kings and common people alike; nor is the modern brown linoleum a very adequate substitute for the original Cosmati floor, the ruined glories of which it is there to protect. But hardest of all, perhaps, is it to picture in the mind's eye the Shrine itself, as it actually was, for the present ravaged and top-heavy structure strikes one very properly as quite unworthy of its actual role in history. Fortunately, however, modern scholarship – in particular the brilliant researches of J. G. O'Neilly – have enabled us to reconstruct almost completely the original form of the Shrine. Both this and the story of how it came to be in its present state are of considerable interest, and can be followed by reference to the picture on p. 45.

As it now stands, the Shrine consists of two parts only: the wooden green and red upper half, in the classical style, and the marble lower half with its trefoil arches and twisted columns and its surface covered with elaborate depressed patterns which were the matrices in which the decoration of porphyry and glass and ceramic mosaic, like that on the altar end, was set. But in fact there were originally three parts, for the top half is not a solid structure, as it appears, but a hollow canopy which once fitted over an ornate casket of beaten gold, called a feretory, containing the coffin with the body of Edward the Confessor, resting on a plinth on top of the lower stone half of the structure. The canopy could be raised and lowered by ropes or chains passing through the vaulting above, to reveal the feretory, enriched over the centuries with many votive offerings in gold and jewellery, to the gaze of pilgrims.

In the course of the Dissolution of religious houses under Henry VIII, the monastery at Westminster was surrendered on 16 January 1540. Within a few months almost all its treasures had been pillaged. The holy relics, too, were destroyed in accordance with the spirit of an age which both the Renaissance in culture and the Reformation in religion had made intolerant of anything which smacked of superstition. But the Shrine called for some circumspection. The Shrine of Thomas à Becket at Canterbury had been ruthlessly swept away without trace; but he was only a saint. Edward the Confessor was not only a saint but a king, and in the inverted but politically vital order of values of the new Tudor monarchy deference must be shown to a king which was quite unnecessary to a Martyr or Confessor. So, although the golden feretory was taken, the former monks were allowed to bury Edward's body elsewhere in the church (no record remains of the spot where it was laid at that time) and to dismantle the Shrine themselves and to store the pieces within the Precincts.

After the death of Edward VI, however, Queen Mary I, who was a Roman Catholic, restored the monastery, John Feckenham, previously Dean of St Paul's, being installed as Abbot. He set to work at once to restore the Shrine as quickly as possible. The stones of the lower half were brought out of storage and reassembled. Since there was now no feretory,

Against the grey stone the banners of the Knights of the Bath blaze with colour. Beneath the windows the ranks of saints and angels have happily survived the Reformation iconoclasts.

Les bannières des Chevaliers du Bath éclatent de couleurs contre la pierre grise. Sous les fenêtres les rangées de saints et d'anges ont bien survécu aux iconoclastes de la Réforme.

Vor dem grauen Stein leuchten die farbenfrohen Banner der Knights of the Bath (Ritter des Bath-Ordens). Die Reihen von Heiligen und Engeln unterhalb der Fenster haben glücklicherweise die Bilderstürmer der Reformation überlebt.

the coffin was placed in the upper part of this base in a cavity just above the side arches. The canopy was then replaced on top, but no provision was made for raising and lowering it, this being unnecessary, since there was now nothing to be seen. The stone cornice which now runs round the top of the base, immediately below the canopy, was new work added by Feckenham. It used to be thought that the canopy itself was a new one, made at this time, but it is now virtually certain that it had been con-structed a few years before the Dissolution. Its design is strongly reminiscent of the choir screen in the Chapel of King's College, Cambridge, built 1534–5. There are two possible reasons why a replacement may have been needed at that time. The original canopy, which had been in use for more than 250 years, was no doubt showing signs of wear and tear,

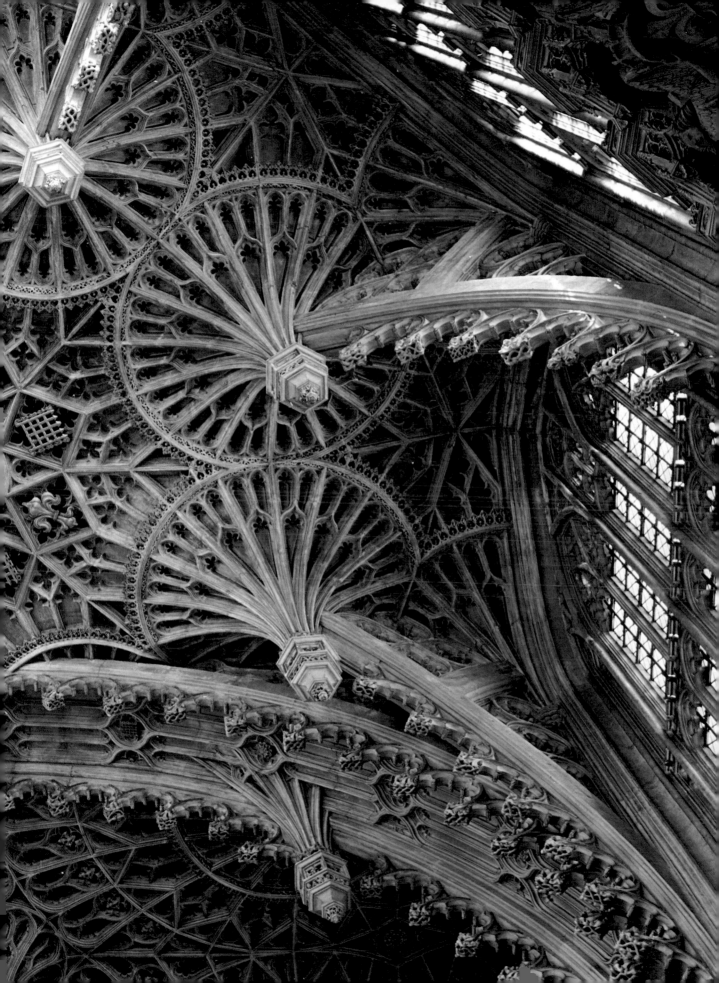

and Henry VII had given a gold statue of himself, in a kneeling position, to be placed on top of the feretory, which may well have called for a canopy of greater height than the original one.

Unfortunately, however, there is ample evidence that the stone base was reassembled incorrectly. First, it was wrongly positioned. There is a blank area in the Cosmati flooring of the Chapel which shows clearly where the Shrine must originally have stood; and from the fact that this area is larger than the space at present occupied by the Shrine it seems likely that in medieval times it rested on a stepped platform. Three courses of steps would exactly fill the room available. This means, in turn, that the Shrine must have risen higher than at present, which again makes sense, for clearly the Screen between the High Altar and the Confessor's Chapel, which was built in 1441, cannot have been intended to block all view of the Shrine from the Choir, as it now does. The canopy of a shrine raised on steps would have been visible, marking the

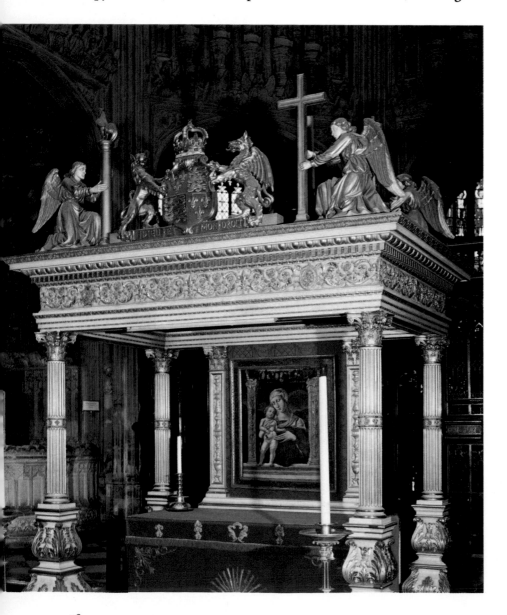

The present altar of Henry VII's Chapel is a reconstruction of the original. The picture of the Virgin and Child is by Vivarini.

L'autel actuel dans la chapelle d'Henri VII est une reconstitution de l'original. Le tableau de la Vierge et l'Enfant est de Vivarini.

Der gegenwärtige Altar in Henry VII's Chapel ist eine Rekonstruktion des Originals. Das Bild der Madonna mit dem Kind ist von Vivarini.

devotional heart of the church. Moreover, if the Shrine were moved slightly eastwards on its platform to leave proper room for the altar which stood at its west end (the present small altar is modern and very cramped), this would bring the centre of the Shrine directly under the mid-point of the vaulting above.

Secondly, the marble lower half of the Shrine was put together wrongly. There are several places where the decorative patterns break off or proceed irregularly; decorated areas which must once have been exposed are hidden by other stones; the designs over the side niches are not lined up with the centres of the arches; a stone worn away where many generations of pilgrims knelt to pray is now in an impossible position for this purpose, and so on. Perhaps most striking of all, the twisted pillars at present supporting the large slab which forms the reredos to the Shrine altar are half buried, which shows that they were never meant for that particular function. The mistakes are understandable. The Shrine had been built 270 years earlier by highly skilled craftsmen. When it was dismantled, not only was there probably no one competent to record the niceties of its construction, but there must have seemed no reason to do so, since nobody

in 1540 can have foreseen the possibility of its restoration. Furthermore, it was taken down in haste, most likely by the monks themselves, and it would be extraordinary if in the process no parts were broken or lost. It is certain that during the next fifteen years, while the Shrine lay in store, at least one piece was used for work elsewhere, since Sir Gilbert Scott discovered it blocking up a window in what had been the monks' dormitory! Again, there is reason to think that the medieval altar has actually survived. In the South Ambulatory there is a Cosmati tomb containing the bones of children of Henry III and Edward I who died very young. The top of this tomb has been cut to force it into its present niche; but its original dimensions fit the width of the Shrine, and it has

decorative markings on its side which match those of the Shrine's marble base. What is more, the presence of a place for relics in the centre of the tomb's top slab shows that it was an altar at one time. Clearly, however, it was impracticable to restore the tomb to its original function; and without it the task of restoration was made even more difficult. The wonder is that Feckenham's craftsmen in 1555 made as good a job of it as they did.

Be that as it may, the fact is that modern research has now been able to recover the original plan with a very high degree of accuracy; and, what is more, 90 per cent of the original materials of the Shrine itself, though not of its stepped platform, are there, even if wrongly assembled. Most important of all, this is the only great medieval shrine of a saint in Britain to have survived the Reformation, and the only one still to have the body of the Saint buried within it. Given such unique good fortune, any other major archaeological feature would surely have been properly restored. This has already been done for the canopy (in 1955), and it is much to be hoped that eventually the courage and the funds will be available to complete the work and to make the Chapel as a whole truly worthy of its history and significance. For this significance is not purely historical; like everything else in the Abbey it has a living and creative force in the present. The Shrine is still a place of pilgrimage – nowadays for the reunion of Christendom. Once a year a Roman Catholic Mass is said at its altar, and there is a growing volume of ecumenical prayer focused through this spot. To restore the Shrine might well be one important way of deepening and extending this new vocation.

West of the Shrine the Coronation Chair (p. 46), on which every monarch has been crowned for the past 650 years, stands where it has stood since the fourteenth century, being brought out only for the coronation ceremony. (It left the building once, when Cromwell had it taken to Westminster Hall for his installation as Lord Protector.)

As we quit the church and emerge into the Cloisters (pp. 14–15), we find ourselves surrounded by a kind of distillation of the whole history of the Abbey. Here the medieval monks spent most of their day, the floors strewn with rushes, the arches glazed to keep out the wind, braziers burning in winter and lamps hanging from the roof. In the South Cloister twenty-six of them who died in the Black Death share a common grave; and on every side of the great square, beneath the flagstones, lie the bodies of many, both clergy and laity, who have served the Abbey right down to the present day. Over them year by year pass the feet of millions from all over the world, wandering here from dawn to dusk even when the church is shut, caught by a strange atmosphere which perhaps they cannot define but which is none the less real and effectual for that. Here they visit the Undercroft (p. 64) and gaze at relics from every period of the Abbey's story and its involvement in the nation's history. Often they just sit on the stone benches along the walls, where once the monks washed the feet of poor children each Maundy Thursday, and look up at the great church, watch the sun on the green of the Cloister Garth, or admire the craftsmanship of the present-day successors of the old masons

The Royal Air Force Chapel, the easternmost point of the Abbey. The window by Hugh Easton commemorates the fighter pilots who died in the Battle of Britain.

La chapelle de la Royal Air Force, à l'extrémité est de l'abbaye. Le vitrail de Hugh Easton commémore les pilotes de guerre morts au cours de la Bataille d'Angleterre.

Die Kapelle der Royal Air Force. Das Fenster von Hugh Easton gedenkt der in der Schlacht um England gefallenen Jagdflieger.

as they repair the crumbling fabric (p. 14). There are no dramatic splendours in these quiet walks, but perhaps the secret of the Abbey is as strong here as anywhere – the living sense that it is eternity which is the real destiny of Man, and that God's true shrine is not in stone or gold but in the humble and peaceable heart.

The Norman Undercroft, which now houses the Abbey's Museum and Exhibition of Treasures.

La crypte romane, qui contient maintenant le musée de l'abbaye et une exposition de ses trésors.

Im normannischen Kellergewölbe sind heute das Abteimuseum und die Ausstellung der Schätze untergebracht.